The Get Out Date:
One Father's Guide to
Raising a Son

The Get Out Date: One Fathers Guide to Raising a Son

By Clarence T. Brown

This Book is Published by CJC Enterprise

Front Cover Photo by George Patterson

The Get Out Date: One Father's Guide to Raising a Son

www.clarencetbrown.com
www.ctb3.com

Library of Congress Control Number:
ISBN- 978-0-9802217-4-9

Printed in the United States of America

clarence@clarencetbrown.com

October 2018

Acknowledgments

I once commented that raising my son was the hardest thing I have ever decided to do. This is definitely true, but luckily, I did not have to do it alone.

To my wife **Consuela**, my partner, my co-facilitator, and the best mother for our son. Without you and your sacrifice and patience, this book would be blank pages, and T would only be half the man that he is today.

To **Auntie Marcie**, T's other mother. Thank you for the sacrifices, love, and support. Also, thank you for always being there for T.

To **Clarence T Brown, III**, the subject. Son, you make me extremely proud to be your father. I know parents should not consider their children their friends, but our relationship defies logic. You are truly my ride-or-die and road dawg. Thank you for the years.

Though T is my first child, there have been countless children entrusted to me starting with my first youth program **Expose**. Thank you, parents, for your trust, and thank you, students (all of who are grown), for allowing me to be a part of your lives and acting as a training ground for Clarence T Brown, III. The lessons that were successful with you, make up much of what has been given to T.

To **the Self-Proclaimed President of T's Fan Club, Takeshia Minter,** thank you for your constant acknowledgment of our efforts and our outcome (T). You rock.

To the multitude of individuals who have lauded my parenting style and encouraged me to share it with the world, I hope this does not disappoint.

CB

Contents

Foreword

The Get Out Date is a fitting portrayal of my life, and the lessons and attitude my father used to raise me. I was born into the perfect storm of my father's life; after his wild days of being a young adult, and before his days of being completely settled into his role as a mature man, ready to give back to the world. This timing allowed me to be raised by a man who had a wealth of experiences, good and bad, he could draw from to teach me, while at the same time, being able to see a man that was still growing, becoming better every day, and continuing to stretch and strengthen his mindset.

My father taught me about integrity and being a man of my word, even when it costs me personally. He taught me how to deal with opposition, and to treat those who disrespect me with respect, without "tucking my tail". I also learned from him that sometimes I will be outright wrong and must first accept the fault in myself, be prepared to "eat crow", learn from the experience, and then move forward.

My entire life, I have been hearing that I have great parents. Having a role model, and a man I could look to in times of need, was truly an essential part of my development. My father's teachings of mental toughness was perfectly balanced by my mother's lessons on emotional intelligence and independence. When I was younger, I used to think I should at least get some of the credit, but I have grown to understand why my parents are rightly deserving of appreciation. I now realize how they have played such an instrumental role in my life, as well as the lives of other young people. It was, and is, truly a blessing to grow under people that are so thoughtful, determined, and intentional about what and how they pour into your life. Also, to have people that truly have your back and best interest at heart. In this book, you will get a glimpse into the minds of my parents, their preparation, a little of the mindset and values that were instilled into me, and how they adapted to all the punches that I threw at them as they worked to raise their' "radical child."

Clarence T Brown, III
The Son

Pictured: Father and Son

Preface

I began writing this book around 2015 to commemorate the approaching due date for launching our son Clarence T Brown, III into the world of adulthood, and to offer some of the tools, tips, and techniques we have used to prepare him for that day. Why "The Get Out Date," you ask? Well, one watchword that has always been our family's creed is Intentional. What this has caused us to do is to always think about each interaction, activity, and word we share with the family. If we were to launch T successfully, we would have to be intentional about the date that it would take place. Just like natural birth, that would allow us to make sure that each trimester of his life was filled with the appropriate nutrients. People remark all the time about how great Consuela and I are as parents, but my reply is always the same. We will not know if we are successful or not, until after he has left our home. Only then will we know if our guidance has been successful. As for right now, we know we have an obedient child. But obedience under duress does not equal success.

This book started as a biography of T's life. But as I wrote, took notes, and continued to experience the lives of him and other youth I encountered, I realized that we had the opportunity to create something more impactful. Instead of simply dropping nuggets and hints, I would be intentional about the advice that I would share. Now, I must tell you that I am very cautious in doing this, because the information shared should only be used to create a personalized roadmap, and is not meant to be your map. What is shared here has worked for us based on T and his temperament, so that is the lens to view this endeavor.

Introduction

The Get Out Date: One Father's Guide to Raising His Son

I really don't know where the idea for the 'Get Out Date' came from. All I know is that it was an original thought that stuck. When we had our son, I knew that my caretaking was over on his eighteenth birthday. Consequently, August 11, 2018, has been heralded as his get-out date since birth. Clarence T Brown, III (affectionately referred to as "T") had to be around the age of two when I first began speaking this date into his ears. Every chance I got, I reminded him August 11, 2018. Honestly, I think the frequency had more to do with preparing my wife than it did with giving him a deadline. But through the years, it stuck, and at some point, I think it became a day that all three of us looked forward to.

Let's start with my childhood. From what I can remember, I thoroughly enjoyed growing up. What I don't remember, is having the greatest relationship with my father. He was in the house, a good provider, provided a spiritual foundation and entrepreneurial spirit, but I don't remember the warm and fuzzy feeling of hanging out with my dad. Not that he was a bad person, this part just had escaped my recollection. As a matter of fact, even as I grew up and left home for college, our fights intensified. I remember a time when my father and I could not stay in the same house for more than a day. But then one day, something clicked. My father and I began to get along. Though it seemed to be suddenly, I know it wasn't. It was a part of a gradual process. Now that I think about it, maybe my father had a non-articulated *"Get Out Plan"* for me.

Since that revelation, I began to see how everything that I am, believe, and share is a result of my relationship with my father. It even caused me to adopt the mindset that God gives us the perfect parents for our journey. And though we don't always agree with our parents or the decisions they make for us, it is all part of a greater plan. Well, as the perfect parent for our son, my divulged plan for his life is *"The Get Out Date."*

1. The Drop-In date (One Day Late)

Thursday, August 10, 8:00 PM, and still nothing happened. It was bad enough that I thought he would be here a few days early, but to keep me waiting all day, that's just insensitive. For weeks, it seemed like it would be any minute now. Consuela's stomach was full and low; the bags were packed and in the trunk of the car, and the car seat was installed. However, as the days drew on, it became apparent that the baby was not going to make an early appearance. So, as the evening of the due date came, I decided that I would intervene. You see, at this point, I could not just sit around and wait anymore. So, I devised a plan to grab a bite to eat, and then go walking. Off to Golden Coral we went. We sat an ate dinner and chatted for a couple of hours, but still no sign of our little one. After dinner, we got into the car and headed to Super Walmart for some walking. We got a grocery cart and walked around and around the store; me, to walk off some of the excess food I had eaten, and Consuela, to rid herself of the overdue freeloader who was supposed to be here already. At 11:00 PM, Consuela was tired and couldn't take it anymore. I was still trying to rush my baby boy to an on-time delivery. However, in what has become typical fashion for our family, we would have to sit and wait. This has morphed into a theme in our lives; wait on T.

Around 11:30 p.m., we leave the store and head home to get some rest. After getting ready for bed, Consuela settles in for the night, but I can't sleep.

Where is that son of mine? Doesn't he realize I have been waiting expectantly for him all day? This was a foreshadowing of days to come. As our son grows and gains his interdependence and ultimately his independence, there will be times when I think he should be where I am, or at least well on his way, but he feels differently. How I prepare myself to handle those days, became a part of my preparation for rearing our son, and ultimately preparing him and my wife for the "Get Out Date." So, as Consuela slept, I sat patiently on the floor, awaiting him to announce his presence by the breaking of water. While I wait, I preoccupy myself with my PlayStation. This also served as a cornerstone of my training to become a father. During my years of raising T, there have been many times where I focused on my own personal and professional development while waiting on him to reach the next milestone in his growth. This prepared me to have more to impart in his life as opposed to remaining stagnant.

It was about three o'clock in the morning when Consuela sprang from the bed and headed toward the bathroom and shouted, it is time. So, just as we had planned, we rushed her to the car and started our journey to the hospital. I don't believe I stopped at a stop sign or red light the entire way there. As we arrived at the hospital, little did we know, the wait would continue. Though Consuela's body was ready, apparently, T still was not. 7 centimeters dilated and steady contractions, but he was not dropping any further. Eight hours later, the second delivery doctor was on shift now. There were some complications he said. No parent is prepared to hear this statement, but for some reason, we were not alarmed. It appears that T had gotten tangled in the umbilical cord. The cord had worked its way around his neck, and the contractions were putting a strain on him. The solution, C-Section. Both Consuela and I agreed, let's get it over with. But wouldn't you know it, we had to wait another two hours.

By the time the nurse finally took Consuela to the operating room, we were about sixteen hours overdue, at least by my calculations. The frustration from this continuous wait introduced my next lesson. The more details I have about a situation in which I am involved, but have no control over, the more I am able to relax. If the medical staff would have communicated the details of the process with us, it would have greatly reduced our anxiety. This lesson taught me that when dealing with T, I should communicate the expectation and the anticipated outcome clearly. Only then could we expect to accomplish what we were after, without frustration. As parents, we tend to try to exact our will on our children, and often, we wind up aggravated. I have learned to enlist T in the process, even if it is from a communication perspective. If the expectations were heard and clearly understood, then we more often than not, wound up successful and in harmony.

In the operating room, everything seemed to go smoothly, until the baby was removed from the womb. First, there was no crying; secondly, they rushed him into another room; thirdly, we saw a team rushing down the hall toward our son with equipment. As strange as this may seem, Consuela nor I were overly concerned. We had waited ten years for the pregnancy and more than eighteen hours for the birth, so we knew God was going to take it from there. And He did. Moments later, we heard cries, and they introduced us to our little one, Clarence T Brown, III. He had problems regulating his temperature at first, and he had to spend a couple of days in NICU, we wound up with a healthy baby boy. And though he had delayed his coming, his tardiness allowed me to learn some valuable lessons, which I have used to raise him to be the man he has become. We have completed the first phase of him getting out. **The Birth.**

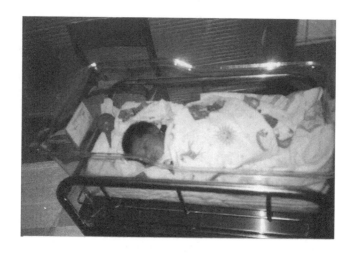

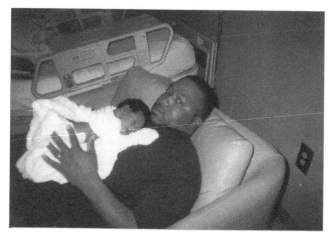

Pictured: Clarence T Brown, III's first days

2. The Early Years

The TV-less Daycare Saga

"No, my child won't be watching Ricky Lake before breakfast." Shortly after my wife returned to work from maternity leave, a relative moved in with us to watch after Baby T. This sacrifice on the relative's part took a huge burden off the family, because we were relatively new to the area, and had not yet developed a sense of community. The only issue I had with this arrangement, was that every morning when we headed out the door to go to work, our provider would come out of the room, grab T, and sit down to watch The Ricky Lake Show. Now, I don't know if you're familiar with this show, but it was one of those early daytime Talk Shows where individuals and groups would air their grievances and share close-kept secrets. By mid-show, there would most often be some huge disagreement, physical altercation, someone being belligerent, or some combination of those. Acceptable television for some, but not quite what I wanted my three-month-old son exposed to on a daily basis. So, the wife and I made the difficult decision to look for child-care outside of the home.

Now, when it comes to taking care of a child, mothers have the nurturing thing down. So, with that, there was a long list of things that my wife needed to see in order to feel safe leaving baby T with strangers. I remember vividly looking for daycares that had monitors, where you could log on and see your child during the day. Then there was the smell and cleanliness factor. However, the one thing I was adamant about was that the daycare could not have a television. Not a single television anywhere. If we walked into the daycare and saw children, no matter the age, watching TV, we would turn around and walk out. Back then, I can remember kids hooked on Barney. It would be nothing to see a toddler throwing a fit because a parent had said it was time to turn Barney off, or it was time to put the child's favorite Barney toy away. One thing I was sure of, was that I did not want our son revering a purple dinosaur to the point that he would pout, shout, or cry. So, our daycare policy was NO TELEVISION. Now, to be honest, T eventually got a glimpse of the Wiggles, and he started watching them at home. But at least we could monitor and control the intake. "Fruit Salad, Yummy Yummy," all over the house.

As I reflect on this time of T's life, it's easy to see why he does not watch much television now. He has had a television in his room since about the age of eight, but it probably has not had more than twenty hours of viewing. Now, he has played his video game system on the television, but he hardly ever takes time to sit down and watch television shows. This foundation was very important for us, because (a) it allowed us to monitor what he watches and (b) we did not have to fight with him about spending too much time in front of the television. The other thing that this did for T was free him up to set and complete some lofty goals during his teenage years. But more on this later in the book. Let's just say, not watching television in daycare increased T's productively, even if by only a little bit.

We have witnessed a lot of children who have been raised by the television. TVs in the home, TVs in the car on the way to school, TVs in school, TVs everywhere. When we witness children, teenagers, and adults acting out what they have seen on TV, I can only surmise that it started by them watching unproductive TV when they were in their formative years. It can be very convenient to have a nanny by TV, but please consider the seed you allow to take root in your child's mind. What goes in, has to come out, and sometimes, we have no choice as to when it does.

The Mother Years

When T was around eighteen months old, we took him out of daycare, primarily due to the fact he was not adjusting to his new classroom environment.

One day, I dropped him off, and he cried profusely. We never did figure out what the problem was, but after two or three days of him yelling and screaming upon arrival, I realized that something had changed about his environment. My wife decided to resign her position to be home with T. I am not telling you that this method will work for you, but it was what we needed. So, for about two years, T hung out at home with his mother.

Starting in the womb, Consuela decided that she would read and sing to the baby. Research suggested this early start would increase a child's vocabulary and academic abilities greater and earlier. So, while at home with T, Consuela would continue this trend. Reading stories and books that would help to expand his imagination and vocabulary. For recreation, they would head to the local park to play. This early bonding experience resulted in a solid mother/son relationship that persists to this day. My wife would fill T's head with positive thoughts about his image and what he was to contribute to the world. Additionally, she would often feed him positive imagery about how he looked. To this point, I often joke with her that she made him vain.

We have often witnessed mothers speaking negatively and berating their children, a sight that has always made me cringe. The time and care that Consuela spent with our son in these early, formative years have provided a trouble-free childhood. T has never raised his voice at his mother, spoke negatively toward her, or showed her any level of disrespect. I have to believe that this is a result of his mother only speaking words of adoration and life into him, well before he was born.

5 to 10 Years Ahead

There has never been a time where I treated T the age that he was at that time. Early on, I realized that our son came as a baby, would become a toddler, then on to the younger years, pre-teen years, teenage years, and eventually adulthood, without us doing a thing. However, what was not guaranteed was his maturity. So, when he was a baby, I talked to him like he was a toddler. When he became a toddler, I talked to him like he was in grade school. I still remember vividly when one of my coworkers overheard me having a conversation with a then three-year-old T regarding getting a haircut. When I hung up the phone, she remarked that she thought I said I was talking to my son, but I was talking to him like a grown man. This was probably true. In my view why teach a toddler how to be a toddler, they have already successfully become a toddler. Instead, I tried to project on T, what he should be like in five to ten years, a successful strategy that I have always employed, and it has paid off.

I can admit to anyone, that I have been T's hardest task-master and critic. But, I can also tell you that I am his biggest and most vocal fan. When the objectives I put out in front of him or help him to develop are realized, the payoff has mostly been huge. To that end, it is no secret that T has always been mature for his age. He has often put himself in the most mature groupings. However, this is not to say he missed his childhood. My wife has always been there to balance my actions with just enough flexibility and leisure to ensure T didn't lose out on life. The goal for this treatment was to get him to a place of processing the consequences of his actions. Because we do know that you can choose your choices, but you cannot choose the consequences of those choices.

Pictured: Clarence T Brown, III and the Mother Years

3. Train Up a Child

There is an often-quoted scripture that says *"Train up a child in the way he should go; even when he is old, he will not depart from it."* **Proverbs 22:6 ESV.** When I became a father, this verse came alive to me. In the beginning, I felt like the action verb in this sentence was **train.** But as I began to watch T grow and develop, and endeavored to raise him "perfectly," I learned that the action verb is **go**, or **the way he should go**, to be more exact. What I realized was that T was sent here on a mission, and as a father, it was my duty to observe him, help him discover that mission, and then equip him with the tools, tips, and techniques necessary to be successful in "the way he should go." As I mentioned earlier, T needed no assistance being who he currently was, but would need a lot of help becoming who he was destined to be. As his father and caretaker, it was my responsibility not to bend him to my will or my interpretation, but to carefully nurture the many paths he would pursue and ultimately the one he would follow. This meant when T wanted to play in the dirt, I needed to comb the area and make sure the environment was free of harmful debris. When he grew up and decided that he wanted to try sports, I needed to be patient with him and provide him with all the tools that would allow him to explore athletics in a safe and fun manner. Finally, when T decided he no longer wanted to participate in sports, as his father it was my responsibility to challenge him to find an area in which he wanted to master for his future. This also meant I had to resist the hyper-masculinity mindset that would cause me to force him to continue to play sports because it was what I did when I grew up.

When T was around the age of eight, I asked him if he wanted to play football. After all, he had tried baseball, soccer, basketball, and karate. When he responded that he did not, I tried to offer to him how safe and fun it would be, and that at his age and size, he didn't have anything to worry about. T's response caught me off guard but taught me a valuable lesson. "Father, I am not afraid, I am just not ready," he said. The importance of this moment did not go unnoticed. As someone who had played football and was waiting for the moment that my mini-me would pick up the pigskin, I wanted to assure him that the timing was right, and the environment was safe. What he wanted me to know was that there was no fear, as well as, no interest. My response to T was, "Son, I understand. Just let me know if and when you are." Again, as a parent, I feel it is our responsibility to monitor "**the way he should go**," and not the way I want him to go. That simple, but profound lesson reminded me of the time when he was three months old in the doctor's office. An older, wiser woman was remarking about how big T's hands were. In my athletic, youthful exuberance, I said, "that means he will make a great boxer." The woman replied, "or judge." Wow, what a perspective changer.

As parents, we all undoubtedly want what's best for our children. We have lived longer than they and have the experiences to help navigate them through life. The challenge is to use this to help them navigate *their* path and not place them on ours, or the one we wished we were on. I have the belief that children are always given the perfect parents for them, but sometimes parents are too slow or unable to recognize their requisite contribution. Though T has chosen a different path than mine, the things I have experienced, both voluntarily and involuntarily, have made for great content and context for him. It takes some swallowing of ego sometimes, but if my ultimate goal is for his success, it is and has been well worth the choice.

On the Road – Father, Hotels, and The pool

Right after T was born, I took a job as a graduate school recruiter. The beauty of this position was that I had the opportunity to travel in and around the state of North Carolina. Therefore, at a very early age, T adopted an affinity for travel. For days at a time, we would travel from city to city, stay in hotel after hotel. As I was off working, T and Consuela had the opportunity to explore the hotels and surrounding city. These trips ultimately played a pivotal role in T's life. Especially since he spent his entire childhood traveling. T got his first passport at the age of nine. The important thing to note is that T grew very accustomed to traveling as an infant, and it has helped him make some important life and career choices based on those experiences.

When I was growing up, we had to wait until the summertime and head to the local YMCA to go swimming. As for T, he had a steady stream of indoor swimming pools by the age of three. He grew up thinking that they were his personal pools. After long road-trips, he would be ready to return to the comfort of his own home, but only a couple of days would go by before he wanted to go swimming in his pool again. As a pre-teen, this exposure came in handy, because when Consuela introduced us to the sport of diving via an introductory course, T immediately decided that he wanted to do it in the ocean. So, when T was eleven, we went to the island of St. Kitts and became certified scuba divers. Since that time, we have made diving in some exotic destination a yearly event. Now, the ocean is T's swimming pool, but it all came about because my wife recognized and nurtured his love for water and swimming.

The Daily Trek – *Walking the neighborhood with our backpack*

One thing I am proud of is that T always seemed to enjoy hanging out with his father. I don't know what it was, but we just always enjoyed the father/son bond. Shortly before T's fourth birthday, we moved from NC to VA. The neighborhood where we lived had walking paths throughout the complex. Every day when I came home from work, T would get his little backpack and take his father for a walk. These walks were the staple of our evenings and set a precedent for years to come. Maybe this was a continuation from our evenings of me playing video games, with T holding the joystick, convinced that he was controlling the opposite team. Whatever it was that developed this foundation, I can say that it was important for the long-range vitality of our relationship.

As a young father, it is not only vital to spend time with your son; it is extremely important to let him choose some of the activities. Only doing what you want to do, ensures that your son will follow you while he is young and feels the pull of your relationship. However, when your son gets old enough to develop external relationships, he will more than likely gravitate toward those who share an interest in the same activities as he, and if he perceives that it is not you, it will be hard to convince him otherwise.

The Layoff. "You should have left there years ago."

Imagine your eleven-year-old telling you that in response to you informing them that you had been laid off from your job of eight-plus years. Well, that was T's advice to me when he came home in June of his sixth-grade year. He always had a knack for saying the right thing at the right time. This experience solidified our relationship and propelled us into the testosterone years. For starters, being laid off from my job gave me the opportunity to eat breakfast with T every morning before he went off to school. The conversations were never really involved or deep, but each day, I would ask him to develop expectations for the day. I wanted him to know that if he did not create expectations for his day, the day would be filled by him fulfilling others expectations. Each afternoon when he arrived home from school, we would sit at the table as he ate and I would ask him about his day, which he mostly answered with "it was good." We never established what good meant.

The one thing that I realized during those years was that I was about to put all of my ideal fathering skills to practice. For the previous five or six years, I had found myself spending more time working and traveling, and less time monitoring and molding. Consuela was there to take up my slack, and we still traveled together two to three times a year, but even then, it was typically a business trip, so T did not have my undivided attention.

In reading the book, *Bringing up Boys* by author Dr. James Dobson, he speaks about the two times when a boy really needs his father the most. The first is between the age of three and five; the second is at the onset of puberty. If there is any truth to this, then I was right on time for my appointment. It was almost as if I had a blank canvas or block of ice and I was about to paint and carve my masterpiece. Starting with T's seventh grade school year, I made it a habit to have lunch with him and his schoolmates once or twice a month. What a great opportunity for me to interact with his peers, his teachers, and his school administrators. Many grew to expect my presence at the school. As a matter fact, some of the kids I met at his school still come up to me in the stores or in the neighborhood to share their life's adventures. Some have even connected with me on social media – an added benefit from the time spent. The major benefit was the continuance of forging a relationship with T. Not only did I do lunch, but I chaperoned every field trip, even one that T was too sick to attend. By so doing, I was able to model for our son one of the principles I have learned to live by, "I am a man of my word, even if it costs me personally." A teacher and assistant principal still follow his life and support his activities whenever asked.

T's seventh-grade year was huge for our relationship. In addition to spending a lot of time together in school and on field trips, we took our first Spring Break Boy's Trip. I am happy to say that these continued throughout his high school years. For Spring Break, T and I headed to Myrtle

Beach for a week. We did not do anything special, but we chilled together. There were a few things that became standard for these traditional trips. First and foremost, they were **boys only**. If we did not want to get up until noon, lay around without washing up or brushing our teeth, or not get dressed all day, it was okay, because it was just us. We spent a couple of days playing basketball, and a round of golf at the Par 3-night course. One night we ate at the Mongolian Grill and ate lunch one day at the Seafood Buffet. Other than that, it was a lot of vegging out while playing video games and doing nothing else. For the two of us, it was perfect. If subjects came up to talk about, we chatted. If nothing was pressing, we did not talk. When it was time for T to learn to drive, we found a lone country road in South Carolina, and he got behind the wheel and just drove. No pressure, no pretense, no problem. These boys' trips were just perfect.

If you have the opportunity to create something like this for your family, I highly recommend it. These occasions do not have to be a whole week; you can make it a long weekend. On this trip, make it your child's agenda and not yours. No pressure, no pretense, no problem. I vividly remember the year when I booked the wrong week for our boy's trip. We got to Myrtle Beach a whole week early. When the resort told us that they only had rooms for the first two days, we had to make some quick adjustments to our trip. In asking T what he wanted to do, his reply was, it doesn't matter, whatever you figure out. How is that for no pressure. We were able to get a room for a few nights, then headed to

Augusta for a few hours to visit family, then off to Atlanta to visit friends. The whole way, T and I were good. No problem. The most important thing about the trip was that we were together. As a bonus, we were even able to work on some real-time, problem-solving techniques. As I see it, my lay-off was our lift-off.

4. The Rite of Passage

As parents, our job is to prepare our kids for the bounce.

What I am about to share is a hard concept to accept I must admit, but I am 100 percent convinced that it is the way we should approach rearing the majority of our children. I say majority because I can also accept that there may be some exceptions. With T, we have done a careful and intentional job of providing a balance of guidance, support, and distance for him to experience and figure out this life that he is responsible for living. While doing this, we also had to be cognizant of areas where he was setting himself up for failure. The greatest dilemma between Consuela and I seemed to be which one of these moments we would approach as teachable moments and allow him to fail, and which of these moments we could use to bolster him up, so it would not ruin or drastically derail his future. Thankfully, a mixture of the two allowed us to make the right decisions for T's development.

Often, I watch parents continue to take on the actions and consequences for their children well into early adulthood, while at the same time wondering why their children refuse to grow up and accept responsibility. Simply put, it is a muscle they have never had to develop. As parents, we have to accept controlled failure as a part of the process. This is the only thing that will aid our children when they are off on their own and have to deal with adversity, especially raising a young, independent-minded son like T. He has always preferred to try and figure out solutions on his own, well before, and even if, he decided to come to Consuela and me for assistance. However, this made it easier for me to decide that I needed to concern myself with the aftermath of T running into issues, than keeping him from running into the issues. Hence the term "the bounce."

No matter how compliant our children are, when they begin to experience freedom, they begin to follow their own whims. At least to the extent that we, as their parents, will not find out. When T got to high school, he found himself spending way more time with other students and teachers than with his mother and I. In so doing; he began taking some of the disposition and actions of those he spent time with. The school and teachers didn't require students to adhere to deadlines; they were not required to do homework, and they rarely even brought home books. I immediately saw this as a problem, because it was developing a pattern that would not appear to yield a good future outcome. It may work for some students, but for the son that I had watched grow, it seemed to be a bad set-up. When T's teacher said that he had an assignment due on Friday, but it would not be considered late until the last day of the quarter, or he did not have to do his work as long as he passed the test (true story), what do you think T did? Exactly. He did what most of us would do, he took the easy route. They even had very liberal test retake policies, that students could keep retaking the test until they got a grade they desired. On the front end, there wasn't much I could do. Even if I forced T to do his work up front, he did not have to give much effort, because the teacher did not have the same expectation as I did. So, my job was to build into T what I needed him to know to recover from the impending tragedy of missing deadlines and skipping the process to get to the result, i.e., the bounce. Watching T, his growing personality and his new environment allowed me to prepare T for the bounce, instead of fighting with him to protect him from what he never considered danger.

ROP 13

When it came to preparing T for the bounce, there were a lot of areas where Consuela and I felt we needed to focus. So, as T approached his thirteenth birthday, we decided to develop a Rite of Passage (ROP) Program that would provide some skillsets and mindsets that we hoped he would carry forward in his life. For starters, we came up with a list of thirteen words, which we termed watchwords, that T would have to define and learn. Next, we researched thirteen things we thought T should absolutely know and know how to do in the case that his mother and I prematurely left his life. This list covered everything from cooking and cleaning a house, to finances, to interacting with law enforcement. Starting on Sunday, thirteen weeks before his birthday, Consuela and I sat down with T and presented him with a binder, an envelope containing his first week's task, and some background information used to guide his week. The following Sunday, we met with T to discuss his week, its successful completion and any challenges he may have faced. For thirteen weeks, we covered all the subjects Consuela, and I thought were important.

Earlier in the book, I talked about how everything that we did with, and for T was intentional, and that I always endeavored to raise T five to ten years ahead. The ROP13 was no different. At the conclusion, we wanted T to be able to move out of our home, and sustain himself by moving into his own place and having a monetized skillset for his provision. The watchwords that we specified would be moral compasses that should guide all his actions and activities.

To culminate the ROP13 experience, we put together a special event to commemorate T's coming of age and to solidify the things he had learned. At this point, we called upon his village; the one that it takes to raise a child. Though Consuela and I have taken a hands-on approach to rear T, there have always been people around him who have spoken positivity into his life and provided assistance where needed. For this activity, I called upon thirteen men who have been instrumental in T's life for assistance. Each of these men represented and displayed the characteristics of the thirteen watchwords given to T at the beginning of ROP13. The men were assembled and situated on a wooded path, each given a smooth pebble with their watchword written on it. T was blindfolded and taken to the trail, where his Papa guided him to each station. At each point, the awaiting man asked T about the watchword and what it meant to him. In reply to T's answer, the men would share a story about why the word was important and how it had played a role in their lives, and then drop the pebble in a bag held by T. At the end of the trail, T still blindfolded, was placed in a car and taken to a banquet hall. Awaiting T to be revealed as a newly transformed young man, were the families of the men and others who have been instrumental in the process of getting T to this point in his life.

Pictured: The Watchwords, The Path, and the Guys

5. Room to Arrive

The words "Room to Arrive" were said to me by my friend Dave Wess during a phone conversation one day. The phrase and that conversation has stuck with me and found meaning in my preparation for The Get-out Date. As a father, I am not, and have not been perfect. This book in no way should be considered my personal parenting bible. However, through trial and error, ebbs and flows, our outcome has paid off. While going through this parenting process, T has been patient with his me and given me **room to arrive** at each place we were in our parenting relationship.

In some cases, this meant me getting it all the way wrong, and him forgiving me. At some places, we were both right and simply just not communicating. But in any case, T and my relationship remained strong because of the space he afforded me.

God blessed me to see Him in raising T and not see me. Being able to see God as I raised my son was very valuable because as a father, it is easy to see how I would handle or react to things and assume that T should do the same. But as I looked at situations, I constantly asked myself, what would God want the outcome to be for this situation. In taking that approach, it allowed me to remove myself and my expectations out of the way, and react in a manner that would yield the result that God wanted. After all, if I am "training a child in the way he should go," shouldn't the Designer be allowed to provide the blueprint? Having this perspective alleviated me of much of the pressure of trying to do the right thing. Inherently, I do not know the right thing for T, only God does. One example of this is in T's football playing days. The team T played fullback and cornerback for, and that I coached, had a record of 4-0. We were halfway through a successful season, and T came to me and said, "Father, if we win the championship, I want to take a year off from football." Now as head coach of a winning team, this was a strange request, so imagine my feelings as a father. Thinking back on my childhood, I would have given anything for my father to coach me in little league football, not to mention, to be a two-way player on an undefeated, playoff-bound team. But, what came to mind was the reason I was there in the first place. It was to support and spend time with T, while at the same time, use my skills to motivate and develop twenty other young men. So, my reply was, "no problem son. Let's go win the championship." The truth is, T never did return to football. He played one uninspired year in middle school but quickly realized that he did not have a love for playing the sport. But, God had other plans for him. Imagine where our music mogul (more on that later) would be if I had seen this as being about me and fulfilling my dreams.

Principles to Live By

A set of my guiding principles include *acknowledging that we are created for a purpose* and **consulting and trusting our internal compass**. These principles have led me to spend a great deal of time introducing T to himself and helping him access that part of him that can authentically guide his decisions. Did I always get this part right, of course not? But using this philosophy still alleviated a lot of pressure from trying to be the perfect father and knowing it all, and it has allowed T to discover and follow a path where he truly excels.

Not the Anti-parent

As I mentioned in the introduction to this book, I do not remember the warm and fuzzy feelings from my father growing up, because what I perceived as negative or bad, weighed more heavily on me, than those things that I overlooked because I expected them. What this selective memory had the risk of doing was making me want to raise T differently from how I was raised. I have seen this done more than enough times to see the error in that line of thinking. Imagine getting into a car to go somewhere, and on the way, the A/C goes out. No matter how uncomfortable the ride, I seriously doubt it would turn you against riding in a car again. The better approach would be to examine the car and only tinker with those things that deal with the car being too hot for you to ride in. Likewise, had I focused on the fact that I did not remember the warm and fuzzy feeling from my father, therefore translating into believing that everything my father did was wrong, I would have endeavored to parent T different from the way I was parented. In so doing, I would be missing out on a huge legacy passed down by my father. As a matter of fact, one of my father's claims to fame is the youth and young adult lives that he has touched. I have adopted that philosophy, and it has allowed me to be a better father for T than had I not followed that example. So clearly, the anti-parent is not the way to go.

Don't let the lesson define our relationship.

Furthermore, I did not always get it right with T, but there were times when I felt as though it was not about being right or wrong. Sometimes it is about the ultimate outcome (in five to ten years). What that really means is that it is about T being proud of, and able to operate in, the place he will inherit in the future, based on his decisions today. With that being said, there were some decisions I did not feel like T was ready to make on his own. For those decisions, I made them for T or better yet, withheld them until he was mature enough to make the right decision for himself. I have witnessed many adults who were given the latitude to make life-altering decisions at a time that, had it been delayed just two or three years, they would have made a totally different decision. The problem is, now they are left suffering the consequences of a decision they were not mature enough to make. One example of this in our family was when T began taking piano lessons at the age of five. He took to the piano quickly, but after a few years, though he showed promise and would go to rehearsal and do well, he would not practice much at home. Being that this experience and expense did not prohibit T from trying other activities, Consuela and I chose to continue him with piano lessons. We did, however, choose to find a new teacher that could move him forward, every time he reached a plateau, instead of allowing him just to quit. At the age of twelve, after plateauing with his third piano teacher, T decided that he wanted to take the time to develop his skills himself. After accessing his maturity level and his ability to follow through, Consuela and I agreed to take him out of the lessons. It turned out to be a very wise decision. At this point, T was able to find and learn various genres of music, not just what was coming from the piano books. His repertoire grew, and he excelled at playing, and at one point, teaching piano. However, if we would have just allowed T to quit after leaving his second teacher and his interest was low, T would not be where he is today. A young music mogul.

Pictured: Clarence T Brown, III after winning the championship

6. The Payoff

T's eleventh-grade year started by attending a brand-new high school. Not brand new, as in new to him, but brand new as in just opened. This high school was designed specifically for students who were interested in the Fine and Performing Arts, of which he was. T had decided that he would like to compose, write, and produce music.

Around the middle of T's eighth-grade year, when he decided that he was not interested in being serious about sports, Consuela and I gave him an option to find something to make his main thing. We intended to have him focus on something other than just sitting around, passing the time in high school. We gave him a choice of athletics, academics, or arts. So, T said academics. This was a great answer, but we quickly added that this did not mean simply going to school. If he truly wanted to focus on academics, we would be finding and enrolling him in academic enrichment camps, and other extra-curricular academic activities. Needless to say, he wanted to rethink the decision. After a couple of days, his mind was made up. He would pursue music. So, in the second semester of his eighth-grade year, we took T to an open house for specialty programs in the county. At the event, we learned that there was a music technology program at a high school on the other side of the county. At this school, students were able to write, perform, and record music for a student-run record label. This excited T. The downside was that he would have to spend two years being bussed an hour away for school. The upside was that after the two years, the county was opening a brand-new school dedicated specifically to students interested in the fine and performing arts, and that school would be only twenty minutes away. Our promise to T was that, if he made that decision, we would support his music endeavors in every way.

The Bridge, The Barracks, or the Dormitory.

Through the process of transitioning to music and looking at specialty programs, we also learned that T was not sold on going to college. Not that he said he wouldn't, but it was the way he was leaning. One thing I had always told T from early in his life, in addition to the "get out date," was that college was his choice because I was not going to pay for it. So, making him go was not an option for me. However, as his father, I needed to prepare him for life after August 11, 2018. So, one Sunday, we sat down and went through an exercise on the minimum amount of money needed to sustain himself without going to college.

Additionally, we discussed what he could do to secure the money so that if his destination weren't college, he would still be okay. The way I described the conversation to T, and to his mother, was that on August 11, 2018, T could move either to a bridge (homeless), the barracks (military), or to a dormitory (college), but that he was not going to be staying with me. Therefore, he might want to take our conversation serious. Before it was all said and done, we had flipcharts and whiteboards out, planning for the next few years of T's life. In addition to the financial exercise, I developed a home compensation plan for T to get him started.

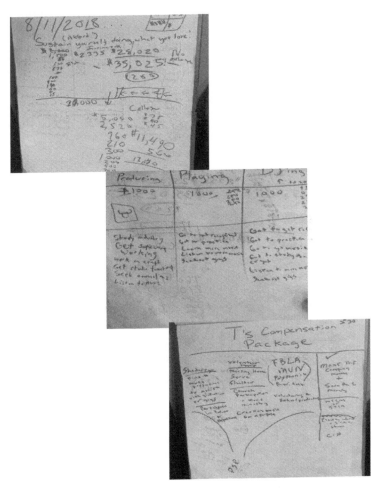

Pictured: The Budget, The 3 Streams and The Compensation Plan

The Compensation Plan

In our home, I have never believed in giving an allowance. The basic chores that T performed compensated his room, board, clothing, and transportation. However, for T's transition to high school and figuring out where he would go from there, I developed a compensation plan. This compensation plan would reward T for going above and beyond in areas of his personal and professional growth. Using a concept shared with me by another friend of mine Alvin Perry, we set T up to quantify his 'above and beyond' by understanding the following categories. The concept says that there are three types of people that work for a company: those that make a company money; those that save a company money; and those who simply implement what they are told to do. If T were to be compensated, he would have to find himself in one of the top two categories. As a part of the plan, we would not compensate T for joining organizations, but we would compensate him for becoming a leader in the organizations he joined. We would also compensate T for volunteering for organizations in areas where he was developing his streams of revenue. And finally, we would compensate T if he found someone in the area of music to shadow and participate in talent showcases. Remember how I said earlier that everything we did was intentional. Well, if T excelled at his compensation plan not only will he have earned some extra money from home, he will have also built his resume and accomplishment for college and scholarship applications.

Three Streams of Revenue.

Above, we discussed the meeting we had to talk about the alternative plan to T not ending up under the bridge, in the barracks, or in the dormitory. The minimum needed to sustain T was about $36,000 before taxes. We had a brief discussion about the number of people who make far less than that per year, even with a degree. But the goal was not to discourage T but to develop a plan that would allow him to be successful. After all, we said we would support him in music. The skills that T wanted to develop for revenue were DJing, Piano Performance and Music Production. To make it easy, we assigned $12,000 per year to each category. This means that by his senior year in high school, T would need to build an income of $1,000 per month from each of his three areas.

I mentioned that T has been playing the piano since the age of five, but I haven't discussed how he started to DJ. The summer before T started high school, we attended a benefit basketball game. At some point, the DJ's assistant passed by, and we struck up a conversation. Being that T was following his interest in music, I asked the DJ assistant if it would be okay if T came up on stage and watched the DJ, to which she agreed. Long story short, after watching and talking with the DJ for a while, T was allowed to try his hand at the DJ rig. Two days later, we bought his first rig, then the speakers, and within a month he had his first paid gig. With that stream of revenue, it only took a couple of years for T to reach his goal. This stream was made possible because as a father, I listened for

T's interest and searched for opportunities for him to explore and excel in that area.

T began playing piano at church and participating in talent shows and expositions, but it was when he entered the eleventh grade at the new high school when he would be discovered. During the first school's concert, T was asked to play for one of the choirs. After the concert, he was approached by a gentleman, who ended up being a pastor at a church in Washington, DC. After some short conversation, and visiting the church, the following Sunday, T was hired as a church musician. The second stream of revenue secured. Now, think back to the decision that Consuela and I made to continue T in piano until he became mature enough to move along on his own. Without those formative years, this move to being paid for his piano services would not be possible. Securing the third stream, was not so simple. It was an area that T wanted to pursue but had yet to begin.

It all started with a chance meeting with a young man selling me a guitar amp. While talking to him at his place, he shared with me his passion for music and even gave me a demonstration of his work. What I noticed in talking to him, and watching what he was doing, it seemed similar to what T was trying to do. Not an exact match, but it was close enough. I shared with this young man about T and asked if he would be open to sharing his story and introducing T to his craft, to which he agreed. A few months later, we connected with the young man, who took T into his studio to show him what he does. A short time later, T emerged and was ready to go. All evening, he researched and compared equipment. A week later, he purchased a Maschine Studio which he began using to create music. With this piece of equipment, T immediately started creating music. By the end of his junior year, T decided that he would use the equipment to create an instrumental album for his senior project. Eventually, this idea morphed, and to start his senior year in high school, T composed music, wrote lyrics, found talent, recorded and produced a full-length album. *First Class: The Legacy* is a 9-track, multi-genre album that highlighted the voices of seven of his classmate's. To introduce the album, T started a production company, Clarence T Brown Productions, signed the artist to contracts, and held an album release party. Starting with his senior year in high school, T had secured his third stream of revenue. How is that for being intentional. There is a proverb that says, "When the pupil is ready, the teacher will appear." For us, "BeatsbyJBlack" was the teacher that came right on time to introduce T to the thing he needed to complete his plan. And, as his father, I was there looking for opportunities to support "the way he should go."

Pictured: Clarence T Brown, III's introduction to DJing

7. The Launch Party

College Ready.

In the last chapter, we told you that T was not convinced that he wanted to go to college. However, we have also told you that we had delayed T making some decisions until he matured enough to make them. With that mindset, we went through the motions of preparing T for college, in the event he decided to go. He signed up for the advanced diploma in high school to make sure he would fulfill all the prerequisites. We made sure that he concentrated on keeping his GPA as high as possible in anticipation of getting a scholarship (remember, I was not paying). And finally, we began taking him to college fairs and visiting colleges his freshman year in high school.

The approach we took on T's college search was somewhat unique. First, we knew that he wanted to focus on the technology side of music, so we only visited schools that had those types of programs. Secondly, we had T research what was needed to secure scholarships from those universities. And finally, we visited only the music department in each of those institutions. We developed an intricate chart on a whiteboard that displayed all the important details, down to how many hours he would have to take in General Education vs. his major classes at each school. In the end, T applied to almost twenty schools, with a 100 percent acceptance rate; and he received scholarship offers from thirteen of them. As a result, T would have viable options, no matter which direction he chose. After all, this is what we ultimately want for our children – prepared in such a way that when the time comes, they have a set of options that are sure to lead to success.

The Grand Finale.

As T's high school career came to an end, he was poised to do some amazing things. Consuela and I had successfully parented T through school in twelve years with no major hiccups. He was graduating with a respectable 3.6 GPA, and his musical talents had allowed him to firmly establish himself as a young music mogul. In addition to being a sought-after DJ, he also was spending a great deal of time with piano performances to include accompaniments and solo performances. He was even contracted to be the musical director for a local charity's Scholarship Gala. After fielding many offers and considering his options, T decided he would attend Hampton University, majoring in Audio Production. By the time he left for college, he had produced and released two albums and a single, and created his first singing group *4EverNHarmony*. Additionally, T had secured enough university and outside scholarships to fully fund his first year of college ($42,000), with all but a little over $12,000 renewed annually. With the help of his mother, T had met his financial goal of putting away $10,000 in his savings account and funding an IRA. He bought his first car with his own money and had become a sought-after producer and DJ. All the while, he has maintained his humility and respectfulness.

Although the "get out date" was scheduled for August 11th, 2018, T decided to leave on his own terms. Prepared, excited, and anxious, he left home on June 15, 2018. And even more fittingly, the day that I would leave our son to start the new chapter of his life was Father's Day 2018. A gift to his father, moving from a state of dependency to a state of interdependency. A gift that I can truly appreciate. Not because he got out early, but because on Father's Day, I launched a man out into the world to continue making his mark.

I have often heard it said that children do not come to us with an instruction manual. While this may be true, I do believe that they come with instructions hardwired into their DNA. As parents, it is our responsibility to use the gift of parenting to monitor and perceive these instructions, and put our children in the right environments to mature them. When the time is right, through a combination of our observations and our children's revelations, our roles will become clearer. It is this combination that allowed Consuela and I to navigate the parenting maze. As I think back over the years, there were definitely times of frustration. But the incremental and eventual pay-offs have far outshined those times. Who would have thought that the young man who made us wait for his arrival, tried to scare us when he got here, and then developed such an independent spirit, would wind up accomplishing so much at an early age? We did. That is why Consuela and I made sure we were intentional. Every time I wanted to give up during those eighteen years, I asked myself, how would this affect T in five to ten years. At that point, I would take a deep breath, pray for strength, and dig back in. It is still too early to see what T will finally do with his gifts, talents, and abilities. But I can say that he has a firm foundation, and is fully prepared for the bounce.

Pictured: Lease Self-termination presented at graduation

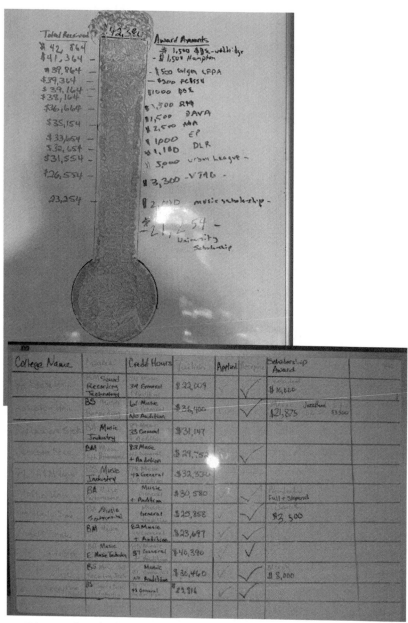

Pictured: Scholarship Tally and College Information Board

Pictured: Clarence T Brown, III signing to attend Hampton

Pictured: Clarence T Brown, III and his company's offerings

The Talk

1. If you have a song that you like, always read the lyrics. If it does not speak life, do not let it speak into your life.

2. Be careful where you lay your money. If you are careless with it in your home, you will be careless with it in your life.

3. Be proud of the number of times you walk away from casual sex, not the number of times you violate a young lady. It takes more of a man to abstain than it does to surrender.

4. Remember the lessons of your youth. Even though your next environment may not understand or support these lessons, they were the right lessons and circumstances to allow you to be sitting/standing where you

are today. Without them, you would be someone and somewhere else.

5. Be careful where you stick your pecker and where you sign your name. The protection of these two things is imperative because violation of them can doom you to ruin.

6. Be seen as someone of quality, with talent worth investing in.

7. Always leave a person/place/situation in a better place than it was when you found it.

8. If you have time to do it wrong, you have time to do it right.

9. You can't outrun your reputation.

10. Adversity is your friend. It is sent to make you, not break you.

11. Everybody that you meet, have ever met, and already know, is going to add, subtract, multiply or divide in your life. Be careful.

12. Don't let your motivation cripple your character.

13. Whoever has your ear, has your future.

14. Be Intentional.

ROP 13

Week 1: Time Management

Week 2: Apartment Living

Week 3: Making A Living

Week 4: Finish It

Week 5 Meal Preparation

Week 6: It's the Law

Week 7: Proper Grooming

Week 8: Lifeline

Week 9: Around the House

Week 10: Serving Others

Week 11: Money

Week 12: Home Alone

Week 13: Street Smarts

Clarence T. Brown

 Clarence T. Brown specializes in ALIGNment, a Five-Step process of calibrating your internal and external resources to maximize performance. Through speaking, training, consulting, and writing, he uses his more than 20 years of for-profit and non-profit management experience to assist clients with ALIGNing their mission with their resources. As founder of The Talking Bout, LLC, Brown uses a unique perspective and a thought-provoking approach to develop training programs and keynote speeches to exceed his customers' needs. Brown also leads a non-profit organization, Pre-College University, Inc., whose mission is to assist individuals with developing a personal strategic plan to enter and complete high school, college, and/or their first and subsequent careers.

Clarence T. Brown is a native of Augusta, GA and is married to his high school sweetheart, Consuela.

They have spent the last 14 years in Northern VA, the backdrop for the raising of Clarence III.

Pictured: Clarence T Brown, III and parents at graduation

The Talking Bout, LLC
P.O. Box 647
Bristow, VA 20136
703-899-8010

Radical Introduction: Beginning by Going Backwards
-Target Audience (Seasoned Adult)
Order: http://www.clarencetbrown.com/store.php

Raising A Radical Child
-Target Audience (Parent/Guardian/Mentor)
Order: http://www.clarencetbrown.com/store.php

Blogs from The Outer Space
- Target Age (All Audiences)
Order: http://www.clarencetbrown.com/store.php

Striving to Be the Authentic Me
- Target Age (All Audiences)
Order: http://www.clarencetbrown.com/store.php

Also at Amazon.com

Made in the USA
Columbia, SC
26 May 2019